W9-BDL-575

Funding for this publication was graciously
provided by the REGE Philanthropic Fund.

Design:
Froeter Design Company, Inc.
Editors:
Kimerly Rorschach and Stephanie Smith

Distributed by the University of Chicago Press.

Library of Congress Control Number:
2003105727

ISBN: 0935573372

Credits:
Pages 14, 16-19, courtesy of The Condé Nast
Publications, Inc.

If, despite our efforts, we have not correctly
identified all copyrights here, holders are asked
to contact the Smart Museum of Art.

David Mazie

TWO VISIONARY BROTHERS: DAVID AND ALFRED

SMART

The David and Alfred Smart Museum of Art
The University of Chicago

On a crisp October day in 1971, a group gathered on the University of Chicago campus to break ground for an art museum that marked the extraordinary achievements of two visionary brothers who rose from a humble background to build a highly successful magazine publishing business. The brothers, David and Alfred Smart, founded *Esquire, Coronet* and other publications in the 1930s and produced educational films for two generations of students. The ground-breaking that autumn day was for the museum named in their honor: the David and Alfred Smart Museum of Art.

David and Alfred were the eldest of three sons and two daughters born to Louis and Mary Smart, both of whom had come to the United States from Russia and settled in Omaha, Nebraska. In 1900, when David was eight and Alfred six, the family moved to Chicago and, like many other struggling newcomers, settled on the West Side in a blue-collar neighborhood.

David Smart's enterprising spirit and charisma propelled him to early business success. He got his first job in a candy store when he was only 10. A few years later he started selling hats at a clothing store in downtown Chicago, soon became the top salesman and dropped out of high school. His next stop, at age 18, was the *Chicago Tribune*, where he began as a stenographer in the classified advertising department, then advanced to the ad sales staff. He quickly recognized that classified ads were cheaper than display ads, so, in a preview of his business skill, he sold advertisers on the strategy of taking a half or full page in the classifieds rather than using a display ad. Within a few months, David was selling more classified ad linage than anyone had previously sold for the *Tribune* and was earning almost $100 a week. But after his supervisors "promoted" him to a regular full-time job at a much lower fixed salary, he quit, and in 1914 set up his own agency for the production of advertising and promotional materials. He made enough money to put his younger brother, Alfred, through the University of Illinois. World War I temporarily interrupted David's rapid rise in the business world. He joined a field artillery unit and served in France. Returning to Chicago after the war, he made a fortune speculating in commodities, only to lose most of it when prices plunged.

Richard (?) Grossenbach, *Portrait of David Smart*,
oil on canvas, 35-1/2 x 27-1/2 inches. Private Collection, Connecticut

Richard (?) Grossenbach, *Portrait of Alfred Smart*,
oil on canvas, 35-1/2 x 27-1/2 inches, Private Collection, Connecticut

Meanwhile, Alfred Smart followed a different route. He earned a degree in engineering at the University of Illinois and, after a brief stint with a municipal agency in Cleveland, returned to Chicago to work in the city's Sanitation Department. In 1921 Alfred joined David to start the David A. Smart Publishing Company.

From appearance and personality to philosophy and lifestyle, the brothers were sharp contrasts. David was short and muscular, with blue eyes, wavy hair and good looks that led people to say he resembled the Duke of Windsor. Dapper and possessing impeccable taste, he sported fresh carnations in the lapels of his custom-made suits. He often was described as "impatient," "mercurial," "short-fused" and "brash." "He could be all of those things," wrote Arnold Gingrich, the renowned editor who spent more than two decades working with David. "Yet his one attribute that comes to mind uppermost...was his unexampled cheerfulness when something really big went wrong. He would try to cheer up the person involved and not make him feel guilty."

Aside from sharing a short stature, Alfred Smart was almost the complete opposite of his older brother. Balding, bespectacled, and conservatively dressed, Alfred brought to mind a college professor rather than an aristocrat. An intellectual who read *The New York Times* and *The Wall Street Journal,* he had a diverse coterie of friends who ranged from Illinois Senator Paul Douglas and the rabbi of a major Chicago temple to famed football coach Clark Shaughnessy.

Long before physical fitness became fashionable, Alfred was a health buff. He did not drink or smoke, and exercised regularly to maintain the athletic ability he had shown as a wrestler and handball player in college. He played golf year-round, using red golf balls in the winter. Unassuming, quiet and modest, Alfred willingly played what seemed like second fiddle, working behind the scenes as David's alter ego. At the same time, his calm, diplomatic approach and pragmatic, tactful style allowed him to implement David's ideas.

The brothers put their complementary abilities to work in a series of business ventures, starting with the publishing company. During the early 1920s the firm sold merchandising and promotional material to banks, haberdasheries and furniture stores. The Smarts debuted in the magazine business in 1927 with *National Men's Wear Salesman*, a trade publication, and then launched *Gentlemen's Quarterly*, an illustrated style book distributed in men's clothing shops. About that time, the brothers added a new, key member to the team — Arnold Gingrich. A Phi Beta Kappa graduate from the University of Michigan, Gingrich was working as an advertising copywriter when friends told the Smarts that he wrote "broad-A English," a talent they figured would add some class to their publications. Over the next 30 years, Gingrich went on to reign as one of the magazine world's most admired and successful editors.

The Smarts changed the name of *National Men's Wear Salesman* to *Apparel Arts* and turned it into an elaborately printed publication that appeared eight times a year. The popularity of *Apparel Arts* — customers were taking copies from stores — led the brothers to start planning a sophisticated, high-quality publication that could also be sold on newsstands. Many rivals questioned the wisdom of launching a fashion magazine for men at a time when only women seemed interested in fashion. The Smarts' plan to charge 50 cents per copy in the midst of the Great Depression — when

The popularity of *Apparel Arts* led the Smart brothers to start planning a sophisticated, high-quality publication that could also be sold on news stands like this 1937 railroad station news stand in Manhattan.

the *Saturday Evening Post* was selling for a nickel — added to the skepticism. The Smarts also planned an innovative and aggressive marketing strategy that called for selling 95,000 copies to men's clothing stores, which in turn would sell them to customers, and distributing an additional 5,000 copies to newsstands for sale to the general public. The 100,000 total was more than the combined circulation of three popular magazines of the time — *Vanity Fair, Town and Country* and *The American Mercury.*

David took a hands-on role in shaping the new publication. According to *Literary Digest,* the fledgling magazine got its name when the firm's lawyer wrote a letter reporting that all proposed names were already copyrighted. It was addressed to Arnold Gingrich, Esq., and David, upon seeing it, shouted excitedly, "Esquire! That's our title." He also tossed out grandiose ideas for editorial content such as having Ernest Hemingway write on fishing, Bobby Jones on golf and Jack Dempsey on boxing.

The new publication was a huge success. *Esquire* appeared in October 1933 with a cover touting "Fiction...Sports...Humor... Clothes...Art... Cartoons." Inside were a "Letter from Cuba" by Hemingway and pieces by John Dos Passos, Erskine Caldwell and Dashiel Hammett. Demand was so great that most of the magazines that had been delivered to haberdasheries were re-routed to newsstands. The run of 100,000 copies sold out. Recognizing that

Apparel Arts, Christmas 1931, first issue.

APPAREL ART

VOL.

MO.

JULY-AUGU

$1.50 PER

Esquire, Autumn 1933, first issue.

they had a success beyond anyone's imagination, the Smarts made *Esquire* a monthly and named Abe Blinder, a University of Chicago graduate who was Alfred's assistant, to be circulation manager.

The Smarts and Gingrich had found a unique formula that produced what *Time* magazine called "one of the most spectacular successes in the U.S. magazine business." In addition to macho articles and pieces on men's fashion, *Esquire* featured colorful paintings and drawings by some of America's leading artists — a combination that Hugh Merrill, the author of *Esky: The Early Years at Esquire*, described as "a mixture of high and low culture." *Esquire* became a showcase for writers of fiction and non-fiction in the United States during the 1930s. Besides Hemingway, Dos Passos, Caldwell and Hammett, it carried pieces by F. Scott Fitzgerald, Ring Lardner, Jr., H.L. Mencken and Bennett Cerf. Probably the most famous short story that appeared in *Esquire* was Hemingway's "The Snows of Kilimanjaro" in 1936. By the end of 1937, the magazine was selling 675,000 copies a month and carrying 155 pages of advertising.

David became the flamboyant real-life model of the Esquire Man. He drove a black Duesenberg and purchased a 38-acre suburban estate overlooking the exclusive Glenview Country Club. Named Willowbrook, the property became the ultimate symbol of David's success, the site of a spectacular Mediterranean-style home surrounded by a pond, swimming pool, stables and greenhouse. In 1942, at the age of 50, David married a stunningly attractive former model named Gabrielle (Gaby) Duré.

Alfred, meanwhile, lived in a comfortable but modest apartment on the north side of Chicago. His marriage to a young University of Illinois graduate had ended in divorce, leaving him

"Esky," the symbol of Esquire Magazine, statuette, h. 24 inches.

CORONET

"INFINITE RICHES IN A LITTLE ROOM"

AND 22 PAGES OF
VISUAL HUMOR

NOVEMBER, 1936
THIRTY-FIVE CENTS

with sole custody of their daughter, Sue. Alfred took single parenthood seriously, attending mothers' meetings at Sue's school, taking her on trips, even bringing home and sharing copies of articles that were to appear in the next *Esquire*.

David Smart had become seriously interested in art on a trip to Europe in 1932 with a Russian-born artist friend, Sam Ostrowsky. The man whose previous art acquisitions consisted mostly of cartoons and pinup-girl drawings talked to curators at European museums, relied on Ostrowsky's advice and came back with paintings by Picasso, Renoir, Chagall and others that turned his office and home into mini-museums.

David's interest in art spilled over to his publishing role, in the form of two new magazines, *Coronet* and *Verve*. As conceived by David, who felt that "beauty is still a very potent market," *Coronet* was to be devoted mainly to art and carry no advertising. The goal, explained Gingrich, "was to make the most beautiful magazine in the world and do it in pocket size." The first issue reflected these aims. It hit the newsstands in November 1936 with a five-color cover featuring an image of a painting from the Art Institute of Chicago. The magazine's 194 pages contained fiction, articles, photos, drawings, etchings and color reproductions of the art of Raphael, Rembrandt and craftsmen from China's Tang and Song dynasties.

Coronet's circulation had a roller-coaster ride in its early years, first soaring, then plummeting. The Smarts tried several tactics to reverse the fall, including cutting the price. Eventually, Alfred found a temporary cure for *Coronet*'s slump when he suggested moving staffer Oscar Dystel to a new role as *Coronet*'s editor. After Dystel took over in 1940, he totally revamped the magazine,

Coronet, November 1936, first issue.

moving it away from the artistic image and *Esquire*-type features. The reproductions of sculptures and vases gave way to warm, homey pictures of kids and pets, and the arty photos of paintings of nudes were moved to a spot where embarrassed readers could avoid them. Dystel's strategies worked, and *Coronet's* circulation started climbing again, eventually topping 2,300,000 in the early 1950s. Dystel went into the service during World War II; when he came out, things were not the same. David had taken over editing the magazine and had decided that it should start carrying advertising. Blinder and Dystel argued strenuously against that, but David was adamant. "Once advertising came, it became a different magazine," said Dystel, who left and went on to a successful career as the head of Bantam Books.

The second attempt to combine art with publishing resulted from a trip to Paris in 1937, when David met Edouard Tériade, the editor of the famed surrealist art magazine *Minotaure*,which had just lost its financial backing. Acting on his love of art and a belief that Americans were ready for "the most beautiful magazine on earth," David entered into an agreement with Tériade in which Esquire, Inc. would pay for printing 15,000 copies in Europe, for distribution in the United States. Under the new title *Verve*, Esquire published the magazine as an oversized quarterly, selling for $2.50 a copy. The publication capitalized on *Minotaure's* reputation and Tériade's close ties with contemporary artists. The cover of the first issue, which appeared in December 1937, featured an original work by Matisse, created expressly for *Verve*, as did most of the magazine's other covers. Chagall and Picasso also did works for the magazine.

In a rare instance, however, the Smarts had misjudged the market. *Verve* sold poorly and disappeared from the American scene in less

Verve, December 1937, first issue.

Ken

APRIL 7TH
VOL.1. NO.1 1938

THE COMING MOROCCAN REVOLT

PRICE 25c PER COPY
EVERY OTHER THURSDAY

than two years. The publishers repurchased most of the unsold issues, but they were damaged later in a warehouse fire. All that remain today are a few bound collectors' copies of all seven issues. Gingrich offered this epitaph for *Verve*: "If Dave Smart had never done anything else in his life but... buy Tériade's magazine, he would still deserve to be remembered as a figure of some significance in the long history of art."

Undaunted by the failure of *Verve*, Esquire Inc. headed in an entirely different direction in the summer of 1937 with a magazine intended to give readers the "inside story" of world events — the news that other publishers overlooked or did not print. After several delays, the new publication, *Ken* (as in knowledge or understanding), reached newsstands in April 1938 as a biweekly costing 25 cents. It carried 50 pages of advertising and articles like "The Coming Moroccan Revolt" and an anti-war piece by Hemingway.

Ken started out as a crusading liberal magazine, a political sensibility that caused financial problems. It criticized big business and the railroads, and supported the rebels in Spain's civil war, a stance that led to a boycott by the Catholic church and threatened advertising for both *Ken* and *Esquire*. In an effort to counter this, *Ken* added anti-communism to its anti-Fascism, which led Hemingway to resign from the board of editors. Circulation began to decline, and by the start of its second year the magazine had lost virtually all of its original advertisers. Instead of cutting their losses and bailing out, the publishers made *Ken* a weekly and lowered the price from a quarter to a dime. When that strategy failed to boost circulation, they decided that they "had backed the wrong horse" and stopped publication. Even in defeat, the Smarts had hit the mark in an important respect: Many of *Ken*'s political predictions

Ken, April 7, 1938, first issue.

and warnings turned out to be accurate, beginning with the Moroccan revolution predicted in the first issue.

Meanwhile, *Esquire* was having its own problems. After reaching a high of 728,000 in January 1938, its circulation began to drop. A wartime paper shortage led to government regulations that threatened further supply reductions, but the publishers reduced the weight and cost of the paper they used, thereby enabling both *Esquire* and *Coronet* to survive without cutting circulation. Also, *Esquire* was one of a handful of magazines designated by the U.S. government as morale boosters in the war effort. Its Petty and Varga Girl pinup art inspired tattoos on the arms of GIs and paintings on the fuselages of bombers.

Not everyone was so appreciative of the drawings, however. In October 1943, as part of a crusade for "clean" magazines, Postmaster General Frank C. Walker ordered *Esquire's* second-class mailing privileges revoked for "obscenity, lewdness and lasciviousness." He appointed a quasi-judicial hearing board consisting of three assistant postmasters general to rule on the matter. Walker cited the pinups — although none was nude — and the use of words such as "bawdy house," "street walker," "syphilis" and "fanny," although witnesses at the hearings pointed out that they were also found in literature and newspapers.

The stakes were tremendous. If *Esquire* lost its second-class privileges, it would face an additional half million dollars a year in mailing costs and might be forced out of business. Virtually all magazines were threatened, so other leading publications entered the proceedings as friends of the court, asserting that "the public should be the only censor." The hearing board voted two to one in *Esquire's* favor, but Walker ignored the recommendation of his own panel and declared that *Esquire* did not meet the requirements for second-class mailing privileges. His decision was appealed to the federal courts, and the U.S. Court of Appeals ruled in 1945 that neither Walker nor any other official had the right to suspend the second-class mailing privileges of any publication on "moral" grounds. More than two years after the initial hearings, the U.S. Supreme Court upheld the Court of Appeals decision, saying, "What is good literature, what has educational values, what is refined public information, what is good art, varies with individuals as it does from one generation to another. The public will pick and choose."

With that threat lifted and World War II over, the Smarts put new energy into other business ventures. The most successful of these stemmed from a 1936 trip David had made to Germany, where he was intrigued by training films produced for the German army. Convinced that film could be used more positively as an educational tool for American children, he built a state-of-the-art movie studio on his Willowbrook estate and started Coronet Instructional Films, the first non-publishing venture of the Esquire company. The new enterprise struggled and produced only a handful of finished movies before the U.S. Navy steamed to the rescue, taking over the studio to make wartime training films. Post-war events helped pump new life into Coronet Films, as Congress appropriated millions of dollars to schools to spur a catch-up effort after Russia launched its Sputnik satellite.

The Smarts guided Coronet to the forefront of the educational film field. They put together a team of actors, writers, directors and cameramen who used Hollywood techniques that included color,

background music and dramatic lighting. In addition, a large group of educators, authors, scientists and other experts was enlisted to help research and develop scripts. Coronet soon began turning out an average of a title a week. In darkened classrooms throughout the country, students got 10 to 12 minutes of 16mm guidance about topics like patriotism, drinking and dating, as well as help with math, history and science. Although the Willowbrook studio was torn down in 1974, production continued elsewhere, and Coronet Films was a major contributor to Esquire Inc.'s profits. For many years, with translations available in 17 languages, Coronet was the world's largest producer of educational films. Their closest rival was Encyclopedia Britannica Films, also based in the Chicago areas.

Neither David nor Alfred Smart was around to savor the success fully, however. Late in 1950, doctors discovered that Alfred had colon cancer that had spread to his liver. He died the following February at the age of 56. Alfred's death was a crushing blow to David, whose distress was exacerbated a few months later when his mother died. In addition, Gingrich, a guiding hand at *Esquire* from its beginning, had gone to another magazine. After Alfred's death, David convinced him to return.

Part of what brought Gingrich back was a promise to move *Esquire*'s headquarters from Chicago to New York, the capital of publishing and advertising. That was a difficult decision for David, who loved Chicago, but he and Gaby prepared to move. During a routine checkup, doctors found a tiny polyp in David's colon. They did not know whether it was malignant, and advised waiting and watching. After consulting several other physicians,

Coronet Films logo, ca. 1950s. Overleaf, Coronet film stills and supplementary materials, ca. 1950s.

however, David decided to have it removed. The surgery was successful and the polyp turned out to be benign. But a few days later, on October 16, 1952, David Smart died from unexpected complications at the age of 60 .

At the time of his death, he owned four residences — Willowbrook; a recently completed home in Boca Raton, Florida; an apartment in downtown Chicago, and a Fifth Avenue penthouse in New York. But David had chosen to be cremated and have his ashes scattered over the city where he had been born, Omaha, where Alfred's ashes also had been taken.

After David died, Esquire magazine had a "rebirth" under Gingrich, and Esquire Inc., led by Abe Blinder and John Smart, the youngest of the three brothers, began a period of expansion and diversification. They bought several businesses, ranging from a lighting firm and a radio station to a publisher of stamp collectors' catalogues. However, in the 1980s, the company began moving in the opposite direction, selling some of its holdings. *Esquire* magazine itself was sold to a group that included *New York* magazine editor Clay Felker. Later, *Esquire* was bought by the Hearst Corporation, which is taking it into its eighth decade of continuous publication with a circulation of about 700,000. *Coronet* magazine and Coronet Films are no longer in existence, but *Gentlemen's Quarterly*, now simply *GQ*, is a Condé Nast publication with a circulation of more than 800,000.

In an effort to use their success for philanthropic ends, David and Alfred established the Smart Family Foundation in 1951. The brothers' original gift to the Foundation consisted of 100,000 shares of Esquire Inc. stock with a total value of $900,000. Since then, the assets of the Foundation have increased significantly, by 2003 totaling over $160 million.

In the early years of the Foundation, Blinder received a request for funding from his alma mater, the University of Chicago. "I realized," Blinder recalled, "that four of our top executives were graduates of the University of Chicago. In addition, the Smart family had long, close ties to the city of Chicago, so the university would be a natural place to give a gift as a memorial to David and Alfred Smart." The university suggested using the money to build an art museum. After visiting the campus and examining plans for the museum, the Foundation's trustees decided to fund it as part of a complex for the arts. The original gift, given in 1967, consisted of $1,000,000 worth of Esquire Inc. stock. The Foundation has since contributed approximately $9 million more for the museum's endowment, exhibitions and capital improvements.

The University of Chicago's David and Alfred Smart Museum of Art opened to the public in 1974. Since then, the collection has grown from 2,000 to more than 8,000 objects, with a focus on modern, contemporary and East Asian art, and a collection of Renaissance and baroque paintings and sculpture donated by the Samuel H. Kress Foundation. Widely regarded as one of the nation's leading university art museums, with a focus on teaching, education and research, the Smart Museum has developed ground breaking programs in art education for a wide range of audiences including school children, college students and adults. The museum is also known for its presentation of groundbreaking exhibitions based on new research by University of Chicago scholars. It continues a tradition of innovation that David and Alfred Smart pursued in their own careers.

In the 1930s and 1940s, the mass media in America were limited to three radio networks, a couple of national newspapers and a dozen or so popular magazines. Magazines, especially, played a far more significant role back then than they do today, since they now face competition from television, the Internet and other new media. The magazines started by the Smarts were among the most innovative and influential of their time, and the Coronet films set a standard for educational films in their day and have become cult favorites in recent years.

Despite their distinctly different personalities, David and Alfred worked smoothly as a team, pursuing their vision of excellence and achievement. As John Smart noted in his remarks at the groundbreaking for the Smart Museum:

"It is fitting that Chicago should be the site of a building that honors their memory. They were always grateful to this city as the place that gave them the opportunity to make good."

The Smart Museum's Richard and Mary L. Gray
Special Exhibition Gallery, with an exhibition of prints by
American artist H.C. Westermann, 2001.

INTERVIEWS

Blinder, Abe. Interview by author, March 22, 2001.

Born, Richard (Senior Curator, Smart Museum). Interview by author, April 26, 2001.

Dystel, Oscar. Interview by author, March 22, 2001.

Elden, Richard (nephew of David and Alfred Smart). Interviews by author, March 21, April 26, 27, 2001; February 2, 2002.

Feitler, Joan (niece of David and Alfred Smart). Interview by author, April 27, 2001.

Feitler, Robert (husband of Joan Feitler). Interview by author, May 15, 2001.

Rorschach, Kimerly (Dana Feitler Director, Smart Museum). Interview by author, April 26, 2001.

Stone, Alan A. (former husband of Alfred Smart's daughter Sue). Interview by author, September 5, 2001.

Waskin, Melvin. Interview by author, November 28, 2002.

UNPUBLISHED SOURCES

"David A. Smart." Typescript biography prepared by Esquire, Inc., n.d.

Guglomo, Richard Charles, and Guglomo, Jane Maxon. "Fleishman/Smart Genealogy." Typescript, n.d.

Kohl, Robert T. Letter to Richard Elden, December 4, 2002.

BOOKS

Anthonioz, Michael. *Verve: The Ultimate Review of Art and Literature (1937-1960).* New York: Harry N. Abrams, 1987.

Gingrich, Arnold. *Nothing But People: The Early Days at Esquire.* New York: Crown Publishers, Inc., 1971.

Merrill, Hugh. *Esky, The Early Years at Esquire.* New Brunswick, N.J.: Rutgers University Press, 1995.

Smith, Ken. *Mental Hygiene: Classroom Films, 1945-1970.* New York: Blast Books, 1999.

PERIODICALS

"Arnold Gingrich Dead." *New York Times,* July 10, 1976.

"Book-Sized Mags for Non-Esquire Minds." *Newsweek,* October 31, 1936, 3.

"Breeches Boys." *Time,* October 5, 1936, 52.

David and Alfred Smart Museum of Art, University of Chicago. *Bulletin* (1999-2000).

"Esquire at 50." *Boston Globe,* May 15, 1983.

"Esquire Banned." *Time,* January 10, 1944, 46.

"Esquire From the Beginning." *Esquire,* June 1983, 13-14.

"Esquire's Kid Brother: Ken Launched as Fortnightly to Reveal 'Great Inside'." *Newsweek,* August 4, 1938, 12.

"Esquire Loses a Round." *Business Week,* January 8, 1944, 87.

"Esquire Wins." *Business Week,* June 9, 1945, 102.

Gingrich, Arnold. "David A. Smart, Esquire: The Renaissance of the Alger Model." *Advertising and Selling,* July 5, 1936, unpaginated.

"Girl with Roses." *Time,* January 30, 1950, 57.

"Ken's Demise." *Newsweek,* July 10, 1939, 37.

"Ken's End." *Time,* July 10, 1939, 33.

Kohl, Robert T. "The Coronet Story." *Esquire, Inc. Update* (corporate newsletter), July 1983.

"Milestones: David Smart Obituary" *Time,* October 27, 1952, 103.

"Petty." Book review. *New York Times,* December 7, 1997.

"Relief for Esky." *Newsweek,* June 11, 1945, 96.

"Saga of Smart." *Time,* May 12, 1941, 63.

"Scribner's to the Smoking Room." *Time,* September 3, 1939, 34.

"Speechless Esquire." *Newsweek,* January 10, 1944, 71.

Talese, Gay. "Dedication." *Esquire,* June 1983, 18.

"The Experts Failed to Blush." *Time,* November 1, 1943, 42.

"To Swell and Back." *Chicago,* September 2000, 145.

"Too Many Magazines?" *Time,* June 17, 1946, 48.

"University's Trove of Pinups Is Admired by All Sorts." *New York Times,* November 25, 1998.

VIDEO TAPES

McDonald, J. Fred, producer/writer, and Callaway, John, host/senior editor. "Those Films You Saw in School." *Chicago Stories* series, no. 134. Chicago: WTTW, 2000.